Lessons In Life for
The 21st Century from
THE SOLITUDE OF JESUS

By Wayne Monbleau

*You Don't Find Water On The Mountaintop
Discovering Nourishment
In Life's Valleys*

*Living In Love
Real Values For A Relevant Faith*

Grace: The Essence of God

Friendship With God

Edited by Wayne Monbleau

The Odes Of Solomon

A New Life In Jesus' Own Words

Wayne Monbleau

Lessons In Life for
The 21st Century from
THE SOLITUDE OF JESUS

Loving Grace Publications

Loving Grace Publications
P.O. Box 500, Lafayette, New Jersey 07848
1-800-480-1638

Copyright ©2001 Wayne Monbleau
All rights reserved
ISBN: 0-944648-60-6
Library of Congress Control Number: 2001091042
Design: Lorraine Nevers
Author Photograph: Vincent Nicoletti

Unless otherwise noted, Scripture quotations are from the NEW AMERICAN STANDARD BIBLE, ©1960, 1962, 1963, 1968, 1971, 1972, 1973, 1975, 1977, by The Lockman Foundation.
Used by permission.

Scripture quotations identified KJV are from the
King James Version of the Bible.

CONTENTS

Introduction
The Strength of Solitude
1

Chapter One
The Value of Solitude
11

Chapter Two
The Father Sees in Secret
25

Chapter Three
Knowing When It's Time to Get Away
41

Chapter Four
Acting Vs. Reacting
59

Chapter Five
To Thine Own Self Be True
75

Chapter Six
Listening For the Unusual
91

"I praise Thee, O Father, Lord of heaven and
earth, that Thou didst hide these things
from the wise and intelligent and
didst reveal them to babes.

Yes, Father, for thus it was well-pleasing
in Thy sight.

All things have been handed over to Me
by My Father; and no one knows the Son,
except the Father; nor does anyone know
the Father, except the Son, and anyone to whom
the Son wills to reveal Him.

Come to Me, all who are weary and
heavy-laden, and I will give you rest.

Take My yoke upon you, and learn from Me,
for I am gentle and humble in heart;
and you shall find rest for your souls.

For My yoke is easy, and My load is light."

Matthew 11:25-30

INTRODUCTION

THE
STRENGTH OF SOLITUDE

*Here is a simple pattern for living
which centers us
and establishes us in peace.*

"When David and his men came to the city, behold, it was burned with fire, and their wives and their sons and their daughters had been taken captive.

Then David and the people who were with him lifted their voices and wept until there was no more strength in them to weep.

Now David's two wives had been taken captive, Ahinoam the Jezreelitess and Abigail the widow of Nabal the Carmelite.

Moreover David was greatly distressed because the people spoke of stoning him, for all the people were embittered, each one because of his sons and daughters.

But David strengthened himself in the Lord His God."

1st Samuel 30: 3-6

"How precious is Thy lovingkindness, O God! And the children of men take refuge in the shadow of Thy wings.

They drink their fill of the abundance of Thy house; and Thou dost give them to drink of the river of Thy delights.

For with Thee is the fountain of life;
In Thy light we see light."

Psalm 36: 7-9

"Be still, and know that I am God: I will be exalted among the heathen, I will be exalted in the earth.

The Lord of hosts is with us; the God of Jacob is our refuge."

Psalm 46: 10-11 KJV

THE
STRENGTH OF SOLITUDE

"In quietness and confidence is your strength."
Isaiah 30:15 KJV

Standing at the threshold of the twenty first century, life has never been more hectic. According to the current laws of survival in our culture, most people's schedules are absolutely full just trying to maintain a standard of living which only seems to demand more and more of our time.

We're all so busy.

Certainly many may conclude that, while they would love to be able to spend renewing time alone with the Savior in the presence of God, they simply do not have room in their lives for this "luxury." Yes, it would seem that the responsibilities and anxieties of present day life preclude our being able to enter into the practice of the art of solitude. Yet, precisely because of this, I believe our need to be centered in solitude has never been greater than at this moment in time.

Perhaps we occasionally hear the still small

voice of God within, intuitively telling us to "slow down," that we *need* peace and quiet in the presence of God. But that gentle word is often washed away by waves of ceaseless activity and the demands put upon our lives. The result is an increasing loss of a healthy sense of identity for the individual. Technologically speaking, our human race continues to make impressive breakthroughs. Yet in the realm of the heart, the discovery more and more people are making is that, in this brave new world, they just don't know who they are anymore.

Through examining the life of Jesus Christ and His practice of solitude, I believe we will see a simple pattern of living for our lives which will center us, establish us in peace, and actually make us far more productive with the use of our time.

Has anyone ever been given a more important task than The Son of God? Jesus came to earth with no less a commission than that of saving the world. We are told He began His ministry at age thirty, so He had a short three year span to accomplish His work: present His teachings, perform His miracles, and perfect the plan of salvation through His own sacrifice and resurrection. And, of course, He did it.

But, what do you suppose? Do you think Jesus was so overwhelmed with His work that He had no time for solitude? Do you suppose

THE SOLITUDE OF JESUS

God the Father said, "Now Jesus, I'm giving You three years to get the job done so jump to it and put Your nose to the grindstone. Make the most of every moment. Don't miss a single opportunity to convey Our plan to the world." Do you think Jesus was so burdened with the problem of atoning for the sin of mankind and explaining the true nature of God to people that He had no time to practice the art of stillness with God?

As we look into the Scriptures together, you may be surprised to find that the Bible records numerous episodes where Jesus purposely got away from the crowds in order to be in solitude. In some cases, even when there was an eagerly awaiting audience Jesus still took off, preferring, or being led to, a quiet place for inner communion instead (Luke 5:15-16). Even if it meant climbing a mountain in the dead of night to experience solitude with His Abba Father, that's what Jesus often did.

I believe we can learn many lessons from examining Jesus' lifestyle of solitude. First, if we see that the Son of God made sure to have frequent periods of communion in silence, away from it all, in spite of the great work He was called to do, then certainly we can, and must, create blocks of time where we too may commune with God in quietness, reaping the benefits of His restoring presence in our lives.

Second, let's be careful not to separate the silence of Jesus from the work of Jesus, as if they are two unrelated subjects. In other words, Jesus' solitude was directly related to His work. His effectiveness was so great because of His quiet and focused Spirit. His direction was clear because He took the time to listen. We will see examples where some of Jesus' most profound decisions were made after He had removed Himself from the immediate pressures of a situation in order to "Be still" (Psalm 46:10) and receive heavenly direction from His Father. Miracles Jesus performed were also often preceded by His having spent a significant amount of time in the communion of solitude.

A third basic lesson to be learned from examining the solitude of Christ is that the focus and quality of *our* work is directly related to how well we understand and practice the presence of God. It's as the Lord spoke through Isaiah, "In quietness & confidence is your strength." (Isaiah 30:15 KJV).

Fourth, I think we can safely conclude that Jesus actually looked forward to being alone in communion with God. He enjoyed it. He instinctively knew this was where He gained His strength from. Hopefully we too will realize that this is where our strength, joy, self-image and direction come from. This is where we experience the presence of God. This is where we gain wisdom, happiness, effectiveness, and peace. King David expressed this thought well when he wrote, "In Thy light we see light" (Psalm 36:9).

In beholding our Savior's practice of being still, *we* are given the invitation from the Holy Spirit to enter in, allowing this same pattern of living to be impressed upon our new hearts in Him. The apostle Paul declared, "If any man is in Christ, he is a new creature; the old things passed away; behold, new things have come" (2 Cor. 5:17). Our old life, outside of Christ, may not have had a single moment or reason for solitude, for a variety of reasons which we will explore in this book. But now that we are in Christ, new things have come and receiving a centering inner strength through communion in solitude with God is one of these new things.

In the chapters ahead we will see that practicing solitude provides us with a life-enhancing set of priorities, a balanced sense of self, in touch with our own creativity and hearing the whispers of the supernatural, as we delight to be in the presence of our Abba Father. May our Savior quicken our hearts to receive and understand all He has for us, as we behold the solitude of Jesus.

CHAPTER 1

THE
VALUE OF SOLITUDE

When solitude is prioritized,
everything else begins to fall into
divine place.

"I do nothing on My Own initiative, but I speak these things as the Father taught Me."

John 8:28

"I did not speak on my own initiative, but the Father Himself Who sent Me has given Me commandment, what to say, and what to speak."

John 12:49

"A disciple is not above his teacher, nor a slave above his master. It is enough for the disciple that he become as his teacher."

Matthew 10: 24-25

"A pupil is not above his teacher; but everyone, after he has been fully trained, will be like his teacher."

Luke 6:40

"I gave you an example that you also should do as I did to you.

Truly, truly, I say to you, a slave is not greater than his master; neither is one who is sent greater than the one who sent him.

If you know these things, you are blessed if you do them."

John 13: 15-17

"See how great a love the Father has bestowed upon us, that we should be called children of God; and such we are.

Beloved, now we are children of God, and it has not appeared as yet what we shall be. We know that, when He appears, we shall be like Him, because we shall see Him just as He is."

1st John 3: 1-2

"And after the earthquake a fire; but the Lord was not in the fire: and after the fire a still small voice.

And it was so, when Elijah heard it, that he wrapped his face in his mantle, and went out and stood in the entrance to the cave. And, behold, there came a voice unto him."

1st Kings 19: 12-13 KJV

THE
VALUE OF SOLITUDE

"And when day came, He departed and went
to a lonely place; and the multitudes were
searching for Him, and came to Him, and tried to
keep Him from going away from them."
Luke 4:42

Jesus didn't crave solitude because He was bored with people or couldn't handle being in the world. No, Jesus made time for stillness because He knew that everything else He was to do hinged upon the quality of His time alone with the Father.

In the first chapter of the Gospel of Mark we are told about the time when Jesus stayed at His disciple Peter's house in Capernaum, near the beginning of His public ministry. Shortly after His arrival Jesus had healed Peter's mother-in-law of a fever and, as news of this miracle quickly spread, "The whole city... gathered at the door" (verse 33). As evening approached, Jesus came out of Peter's house and performed numerous healings. Many were delivered of evil spirits and the result was that all were astounded

THE VALUE OF SOLITUDE

by the power Jesus possessed.

What was Jesus' response to this sudden popularity? Beginning in verse 35 the Scripture says, "And in the early morning, while it was still dark, He arose and went out and departed to a lonely place, and was praying there. And Simon and his companions hunted for Him; and they found Him, and said to Him, 'Everyone is looking for You.' And He said to them, 'Let us go somewhere else to the towns nearby, in order that I may preach there also; for that is what I came out for.'"

Why had the entire city come out to Jesus? Was it to hear Him preach and to understand His message? Were they turning their hearts in repentance to the Lord? No, that wasn't it. They had come to Him because they wanted something from Him, and what they wanted was His healing power. Jesus said He came to preach the message of the Gospel but these folks only had ears to hear about His miracle power.

What was Jesus to do? Should He just "go with the flow" and allow Himself to be pressured into giving the people what they wanted? Of course not. Jesus knew why He had come and He knew what He had to do. So, He got alone, away from everyone, and communed in solitude with His Father about this matter.

When Peter and his friends finally caught up with Jesus, they responded to His early morning disappearing act with their own natural logic. "Are you crazy Jesus? Everybody is looking for you. You've got a captive audience back in Capernaum and you come out here where there's nobody? What's the matter with you? You'll never change the world with this kind of attitude."

They just didn't understand Jesus' priorities.

Apparently the disciples figured that the most important thing to do was to 'wow' the crowds with impressive displays of miracle power. Then, when you have their attention, you can preach if you want to. But being out here alone in the wilderness was nuts as far as they were concerned.

Despite their admirable enthusiasm, the disciples often seemed to be way out of step with Jesus. Peter, in particular, frequently thought he knew what Jesus should do. And Jesus would continually confound them all by doing something else. Simply put, the disciples had a different set of priorities than Jesus in this instance. Their thinking was, at this point in time, more in step with that of the world. To them it was: #1 - Miracles and mighty acts - get the people's attention, and then #2 - Preaching, and #3 - Time alone with God, which they did not yet understand or appreciate.

However, Jesus made his own priorities absolutely clear in this instance. In doing so

He presented a blueprint for living to His disciples, and to us. Jesus' priorities were: #1 - Time alone with God - He got up early specifically to commune with His Father, #2 - Preaching and #3 - Miracles. You see, the disciples' priorities were completely the opposite.

Jesus knew the people of Capernaum were missing the point of His power. That's why He left town. Sure, He could have stayed and healed them all day long but they never would have understood His true purpose. So, Jesus got up early the next morning, while it was still dark, and He began His day in solitude with God. By the time the disciples found Him, Jesus had received, in His stillness, the direction He sought. The answer to this situation was to simply leave it for now and go somewhere else. Jesus had come as God's only begotten Son to preach the message of the kingdom of God, not to be stereotyped as being a miracle worker and healer.

To Peter and the rest of the disciples, this was sheer folly. They saw things differently. They figured Jesus should grab the opportunity to minister to the crowd in Capernaum. The big difference here though is that Jesus actually *prayed* about what to do, One on One with God, while the disciples *assumed* they already knew what should be done.

THE SOLITUDE OF JESUS

When Christian services are advertised these days, it's frequently the miracles that are touted the loudest. It's miracles first and foremost, then perhaps a message, and probably no mention of time alone with God. Perhaps we are guilty of walking in the logic of the disciples. Instead of developing an intimate relationship with God through the practice of solitude, it may be that the art of stillness has been lost to this generation of Christianity.

May we all learn from our Savior on this matter.

Jesus performed the greatest work of all time, and I am convinced His obedience to His Father was successful and complete because He always kept His priorities straight. First came time alone with God. If the day was to be a busy one, He would apparently get up a little earlier. But no matter what, He did not forego communion in quietness with the Father. In this environment He was able to clearly hear what He was to do that day. I believe this is part of the meaning of Jesus' frequent statements throughout the Gospel of John such as, "The Son can do nothing of Himself, unless it is something He sees the Father doing" (John 5:19) and "I can do nothing on my own initiative. As I hear, I judge" (John 5:30).

Preaching was next. This was the most important part of Jesus' ministry to people. In the case of the Capernaum crowd, they really were not there to hear Him so, as Jesus spent time in solitude considering this matter, He realized he had to go somewhere else. Even though they were receptive to His miracles and *seemed* eager to hear, Jesus understood that, in their hearts, they were more interested in what they could get from God than they were in really listening to His message. Perhaps leaving them for awhile would give them time to think about His true purpose, message of salvation and the meaning of His presence among them.

Third on Jesus' list of priorities were the miracles. They were to bear witness to His message. I think Jesus recognized that, in the town of Capernaum, the miracles had become the message and that's why He was led to go somewhere else.

In today's works-oriented Christianity, perhaps Jesus' lifestyle doesn't make much sense. If it doesn't, it's most likely because Jesus' lifestyle was based upon His practice of communion with God. I'm sure anyone could reason away Jesus' priority of putting stillness first. It's all too easy to convince ourselves that *our* needs and priorities have changed along with the times. I believe it takes a simple childlike faith and a humble heart approach in order for us to begin to desire to walk the same path Jesus walked. "It is enough for the disciple that he

THE SOLITUDE OF JESUS

become as his teacher" Jesus said, indicating His desire for us to follow the example of His life (Matthew 10:25).

Here's the practical benefit for us as we learn to value solitude: entering the presence of God in stillness enables us to hear His voice. Just as Jesus received direction for His ministry from His Father that early morning in prayer, so we, too, can hear God's voice of guidance and wisdom for our lives as we allow our relationship with Him to be strengthened in solitude.

It's like the account of Elijah the prophet, recorded in the nineteenth chapter of the Old Testament book of First Kings. Hiding out in a cave in the wilderness, fearing wicked queen Jezebel's decree to have him killed, Elijah needed to know what to do. He was in despair. He thought everyone was against him. It was here in the solitude of the wilderness that the voice of the Lord came to Elijah. Scripture says, "And behold, the Lord was passing by! And a great and strong wind was rending the mountains... but the Lord was not in the wind. And after the wind an earthquake, but the Lord was not in the earthquake. And after the earthquake a fire, but the Lord was not in the fire; and after the fire a sound of a gentle blowing. And it came about when Elijah heard it, that he wrapped his face in his mantle, and went out and stood in the entrance of the cave. And behold, a voice came to him and said, 'What are you doing here, Elijah?'" (Verses 11-13).

God was not in the strong wind, the earthquake or the fire. But He was in the gentle blowing. When Elijah heard that gentle sound, he was drawn out of his cave. He wrapped his face in his mantle (his mantle represented God's anointing upon him, as when he passed his mantle on to his apprentice Elisha), went out of the cave, and heard the voice of God, giving direction to his life.

It's the same for us. As we learn to appreciate God's gentle voice in stillness we, too, are drawn out of caves of fear, anxiety and ceaseless activity. We can wrap our face in our mantle, begin seeing ourselves the same way God sees us, and go forth to Him, out of our caves and into His presence. Solitude enables us to see our true identity in the anointing He has given us as His beloved children (1st John 3:2). He speaks gently so we may learn to appreciate being still. And then, the comfort, wisdom and guidance God gives us in His gentle blowing becomes the message we can proclaim to the world around us. "What you hear whispered in your ear, proclaim upon the housetops" Jesus said (Matthew 10:27).

Let us trust in God's wisdom and priorities. Let us place stillness first in our lives. Even if it doesn't seem to make sense to someone right now, at the very least, everyone ought to be able to see Jesus' order of priorities and recognize the fruitful result of them in His work. Hopefully we will also receive the exhortation and encouragement through His life for us to walk in this same way.

Let me repeat once more that the effectiveness of Jesus cannot and must not be separated from the solitude of Jesus. With a new determination on our part, let us pray for God's wisdom and leading so we may follow the priorities of Jesus, no matter what others may think or say. As we begin to practice the solitude of Christ, we will also begin to experience the benefits of God's personal direction for our lives.

Agreeing in our heart with Jesus' priorities tunes our spirit to the frequency of His presence, in stillness, and begins revealing the many blessings that are ours as we joyfully learn to build our relationship with God through quiet times of renewing communion with our Lord.

CHAPTER 2

THE
FATHER SEES IN SECRET

Here's where our joy is,
living our life from the secret place.

"He stretched out His hand and touched him, saying, 'I am willing; be cleansed.' And immediately his leprosy was cleansed.

And Jesus said to him, 'See that you tell no one.'"

Matthew 8: 3-4

"He touched their eyes, saying, 'Be it done to you according to your faith.'

And their eyes were opened. And Jesus sternly warned them, saying, 'See here, let no one know about this!'"

Matthew 9: 29-30

"Taking the child by the hand, He said to her, 'Talitha kum!' (Which translated means, 'Little girl, I say to you, arise!').

And immediately the girl rose and began to walk; for she was twelve years old. And immediately they were completely astounded.

And He gave them strict orders that no one should know about this."

Mark 5: 41-43

"Looking up to heaven with a deep sigh, He said to him, 'Ephatha!' that is, 'Be opened!'

And his ears were opened, and the impediment of his tongue was removed, and he began speaking plainly.

And He (Jesus) gave them orders not to tell anyone."

Mark 7: 34-36

"If any man is thirsty, let him come to Me and drink.

He who believes in Me, as the Scripture said, 'From his innermost being shall flow rivers of living water.'"

John 7: 37-38

THE
FATHER SEES IN SECRET

"When you give alms, do not let your left hand know what your right hand is doing that your alms may be in secret; and your Father Who sees in secret will repay you."

"When you pray, go into your inner room, and when you have shut your door, pray to your Father Who is in secret, and your Father Who sees in secret will repay you."

"When you fast, anoint your head, and wash your face so that you may not be seen fasting by men, but by your Father Who is in secret; and your Father Who sees in secret will repay you."
    Matthew 6: 3-4, 6, 17-18

If you have been led to believe the main reason God drew you to Himself was for the work you must do for Him, then Jesus' priorities for life may be a bit hard to accept at first. Perhaps you were never specifically told that, not in those words anyway, but the "saved-to-serve" mentality certainly is regarded by many to be a virtue and is unquestioningly accepted in much of today's Christianity.

If every message you hear revolves around *your* service, *your* works, and *your* spotless performance, then you might easily conclude that God is more interested in how well you serve Him than He is in developing an intimate union and relationship with you. In this type of environment, you won't be encouraged to grow into a healthy, balanced life of quietness in God's presence. If you are constantly being bombarded with one message after another telling you to be more, give more, serve more and obey more, the basic understanding in this exteriorly oriented, and therefore superficial, gospel is that working for the kingdom is what matters most. Spirituality is defined by how well one prays, witnesses, serves, obeys, attends services and reads the Bible rather than being defined by the quality and understanding of an inward life with God.

In the course of His sermon On The Mount, recorded in chapters five through seven of Matthew's Gospel, Jesus spoke about the values of our heavenly Father. If we can recognize and accept our Father's values then the priorities of Jesus will come into an even clearer focus for us. The truth Jesus shares with us repeatedly is that our Father places a high value upon acts done in private, for Him alone to see and reward, while deeds of charity done for all to behold receive little or no recognition

THE SOLITUDE OF JESUS

from Him at all!

How contrary our Father's way of thinking is when compared to current thinking in much of today's Christianity. We have been conditioned to believe that good works done or miracles claimed should get big headlines so the most people possible may see and believe. We unquestioningly accept the premise that numbers (and the support that numbers bring) count and, therefore, often the individual feels he or she does not count. Outer conduct is stressed almost exclusively while the inner life, where true values and the love of God are realized, is often ignored. The first and greatest commandment of some's faith seems to be "Bigger is better," which has a second likened unto it, "Get the maximum exposure."

It is precisely this way of thinking that has made communion in Christ an all but forgotten art. If we allow our spiritual values to be fashioned on the basis of what man sees, we will really have no other choice but to continue living in bondage to the opinion and approval of people. However, as you examine God's value system and hear the call of the Father for you to live in secret with Him, I believe your inner life in Christ will blossom, filling you with the joy of His presence. This realization of His Life within will gradually grow outward, influencing your entire being in a healthy, centered and fruitful way.

Let's take a close look at a few verses from Matthew so we may see the "what" and "why" of God's value system. In chapter 6, beginning at verse 3, Jesus said, "When you give alms, do not let your left hand know what your right hand is doing that your alms may be in secret; and your Father who sees in secret will repay you." I heard someone once remark that the meaning of Jesus saying not to let your left hand know what your right hand is doing is that you need two hands to count your money. Now this is what I call keeping a secret - when you don't even let yourself know what you are doing. You just pull the money out of your pocket and give.

Instead of giving a gift in order to be recognized or thanked by people, or have our name engraved on a plaque, Jesus said, "When therefore you give alms, do not sound a trumpet before you, as the hypocrites do in the synagogues and in the streets, that they may be honored by men. Truly I say to you, they have their reward in full" (Matthew 6:2). Jesus performed a bit of psychology here. He was saying that this desire of ours to have everybody know about our good works is not, at its heart, to glorify God. Rather it's actually a form of being in bondage. This is about being in bondage to the opinions and approval of others. When we live this way, all of our focus is upon how accepted we feel by

THE SOLITUDE OF JESUS

others, and we entirely miss out on our inner life. But if we will learn the surpassing value of doing good for others that only our Lord can see, then we will be *freed from* the bondage of seeking other's attention and approval and *freed into* the experience of the joy of communing with our Father in secret.

There is, of course, a time and a place for public good works, but it's our heart attitude that's the issue here. The Son of God performed many of His miracles before great crowds but these public displays of power were the exception to His rule of acting quietly and compassionately in a one-on-one setting, far away from the noise of the throngs. When Jesus ministered to someone, He had that individual in mind. His focus was upon the person in need, not upon the reaction of the multitude. Jesus didn't time His acts to be seen by men. He was simply doing the work of His Father. The heart of Christ was completely free from all self-consciousness and the need for self-glory.

What about us? Is our eye singly upon our Father Who sees in secret or is it upon the crowd? Are we serving because we love God and have been changed into His image or are we serving out of compulsion, or guilt, or because of our insecurities?

Let's see what else Jesus said about living in secret. "When you pray, go into the inner room, and when you have shut the door, pray to your Father who is in secret, and your Father who sees in secret will repay you" (Matthew 6:6). Once more God is calling us to the interior life. Don't let anyone hear you pray. Make sure your door is shut. Perhaps you're thinking, "What's the big deal? Why is it so important to be alone when I pray?"

Why is solitude so important? Why does our Father place such a high priority upon our development of one-on-one time alone with Him? Why does Jesus encourage us to give and pray in private, away from the crowds? The answer is simple. God knows it will only be when the eye of our heart is solely upon Him, with no thought for the opinion of others, that we will at last be free to begin understanding His true nature and values. This in turn will bring us into the experience of the river of His living water flowing out of our innermost being (John 7:38).

When we are willing to leave the multitudes behind in order to come alone, gratefully, into His presence, that's when the peace that passes understanding, the joy unspeakable and full of glory, and the actual abundant life of Christ are realized in our lives. When our relationship and union with Jesus Christ and our Abba Father becomes the primary focus of our lives, then we will be knowing Him as He truly is.

THE SOLITUDE OF JESUS

If you love God more than you love the approval of people, then your delight will be in knowing you have done something out of a pure response to His love and presence in your life. Your heart will say "It is enough that my Lord knows" and you will be glad within that you can honestly make that declaration.

I believe our Father is blessed when we reflect His love to someone for no other reason than this is simply what we want to do. The sign we have truly received and understood His love is seen when we begin living in and giving out His love, without conditions, or self-consciousness and without an audience. Living in secret frees us from giving to impress our peers and we're also freed from playing the game of glorifying God as long as we get to be in the spotlight too. Here's where our joy is, living our life from the secret place. This is the attitude Jesus possessed while He was upon the earth and that's why He delighted to be in secret with His Father in solitude.

Throughout the Gospels there are numerous accounts where Jesus healed individuals and said to them, "Go, and tell no one" (Matt. 8:4, 9:30, & 12:16 are just a few). Jesus had only one thing in His heart and that was to always do His Father's will. With that as His goal it makes perfect sense that Jesus would do His works without caring at all about what kind of "testimony mileage" He got. Because His relationship with His Father was in the right place, the Son of God gave, prayed, and healed with no thought of being acknowledged by men. More than anyone, Jesus knew the surpassing value and strength that comes from living a simple and uncomplicated life in secret.

As long as we care more about the opinion of man than the opinion of God, we rob ourselves of the awareness of our intimate relationship with our "Abba" Father. As long as we live our life on the outside, a superficial existence based upon rules, rather than a life in secret generated from a heart of love, we will never be able to fully experience the abundant life Jesus promised. The natural man will never live by God's values and will, consequently, never know what he has been missing.

The Father sees in secret. God is longing for us to meet Him in the secret place of our heart. He is waiting. He is calling. Are we listening?

In the seventeenth verse of Matthew six, Jesus said, "When you fast, anoint your head, and wash your face so that you may not be seen fasting by men, but by your Father who is in secret; and your Father who sees in secret will repay you." There's something important here, something Jesus also mentioned in the previous passage

THE SOLITUDE OF JESUS

about prayer. Concerning the giving of alms, Jesus said, "Your Father who SEES in secret." But in the passage about prayer and in this verse He adds, "Your Father WHO IS in secret." This is the key. God says to give, pray, and fast in secret because THAT IS WHERE HE IS. If you want to experience His presence, then meet Him in secret, for that is where He is. It's so beautifully simple, really. God is telling us right where He is and how we can meet Him there anytime.

By allowing your life and values to be in accord with your Savior, you are choosing to live in secret with your Father. As long as you do things to be seen and recognized by men, you do them apart from your Father. But when your heart's desire is changed and you begin to give, pray, and fast in secret, to be seen only by God, for the unique joy of knowing that when you do something in secret you are actually doing it for your Father, then your oneness with God becomes your daily focus and joy.

When you give, I encourage you to give in secret. God is your source of supply. Let your joy be in knowing your giving is in response to all He gives you in secret.

When you pray, make your requests known to God and give Him a chance to divinely answer you. This will increase your faith in Him and your communication with

Him.

When you fast, don't let others know about it. Instead of being dramatic or self-absorbed about your deprivation, live with the eye of your heart upon the Lord, knowing His goodness is your deliverance from every burden.

Each of these practices point directly to a life with solitude as the number one priority. I cannot emphasize enough what an affront this concept of living in secret is to the natural way of doing things. If we are threatened by this kind of lifestyle, it is probably because there is nothing in it to bolster our ego or give an approval-based motivation for living the Christian life.

Someone may say, "If everybody were to act this way, where would our testimony be?" to which I reply, if everybody were to act this way the whole world just might become Christian. If we performed an act of kindness and the recipient of this act were to see we were simply loving, with no thought of acknowledgment, I am convinced this person would have a favorable impression of Christianity. If we all lived according to these values, the world would have no other choice but to sit up and take notice concerning the substance of our faith. You know as well as I do that this unbelieving world currently looks at Christianity as a superficial religion, out to pick people's pockets and control their lives. However, if we will begin living the inner life in secret with our Father, giving out to others according to inner life values, pretty soon Christianity will gain a renewed reputation for being real and I can't help but believe this will have a major impact upon the world in which we live.

The beautiful paradox is, as we dedicate ourselves to a life of joyful living in secret, for our Father's eyes only, very soon all men may know and glorify God.

CHAPTER 3

KNOWING WHEN IT'S TIME TO GET AWAY

This is a holy self-awareness that balances
our life between activity and solitude.

"And the apostles gathered together with Jesus; and they reported to Him all that they had done and taught.

And He said to them, 'Come away to a lonely place and rest a while.' (For there were many people coming and going, and they did not even have time to eat.)

And they went away in the boat to a lonely place by themselves."
Mark 6: 30-32

"Now as they were traveling along, He entered a certain village; and a woman named Martha welcomed Him into her home.

And she had a sister called Mary, who moreover was listening to the Lord's word, seated at His feet.

But Martha was distracted with all her preparations; and she came up to Him, and said, 'Lord, do You not care that my sister has left me to do all the serving alone? Then tell her to help me.'

But the Lord answered and said to her, 'Martha, Martha, you are worried and bothered about so many things;

But only a few things are necessary, really only one, for Mary has chosen the good part, which shall not be taken away from her.'"
Luke 10: 38-42

"I am the vine, you are the branches; he who abides in Me, and I in him, he bears much fruit; for apart from Me you can do nothing."
John 15:5

KNOWING WHEN IT'S TIME TO GET AWAY

"Great multitudes were gathering to hear Him
and to be healed of their sicknesses.
But He Himself would often slip away
to the wilderness to pray."
Luke 5: 15-16

A life without solitude is an unbalanced life.

Imagine that our solitude with God is the hub of a wheel, the hub of the wheel of our life. Our hub of inner communion supports and directs all of the intricately woven spokes of our being. When we are still, we know He is our God, the Creator and Sustainer of our lives, and we experience a healthy balance coming from within.

If we are not still, we lose our hub, that sense of centeredness, and we begin to drift, having only our own feelings or the opinions of others to fall back on. Consequently, our lives may feel more like we're living with chaos rather than with the Prince of Peace.

In the 5th chapter of Luke's Gospel, we are told about a time when Jesus let a great opportunity for ministry pass Him by. Apparently the hub of His wheel was sending Him in a different direction than the one that the multitudes were expecting of Him. Beginning in verse twelve, the Scripture says, "Behold, there was a man full of leprosy; and when he saw Jesus, he fell on his face and implored Him, saying, 'Lord, if You are willing, You can make me clean.' And He stretched out His hand and touched him, saying, 'I am willing, be cleansed.' And immediately the leprosy left him. And He ordered him to tell no one, 'But go and show yourself to the priest, and make an offering for your cleansing, just as Moses commanded, for a testimony to them.' But the news about Him was spreading even farther, and great multitudes were gathering to hear Him and to be healed of their sicknesses. But He Himself would often slip away to the wilderness and pray" (Luke 5: 12-16).

This last verse, about Jesus slipping away from an eagerly awaiting crowd, might be hard to accept, particularly if you've been made to feel you have got to meet every need every time no matter what. We've examined Jesus' value system and have seen that being alone in quietness with God was a top priority for Him. It was His delight, His time of restoration. We have also seen how Jesus' solitude was directly related to His work. Jesus rejoiced to do His Father's will, but He was still first, and in His stillness He was able to *hear* His Father's will. Jesus' priorities were in order. His fruitful actions were born out of His fruitful communion.

In this passage from Luke we see a classic example of an open door for ministry. Jesus had healed a leper and, as a result, "great multitudes were gathering to hear Him and to be healed of their sicknesses." What did Jesus do with this apparently wonderful opportunity and, even more importantly, *why* did He do what He did?

What if it were us in this situation? I bet most of us would succumb to the feeling of obligation to stay and minister to the crowd, assuming this is what God would want, regardless of how tired and worn out we may be. After all, the Bible says these people wanted to hear Jesus. They didn't just come for healing, although healing was certainly on their minds. And yet, given these circumstances, the concluding verse in this account says, "But He Himself would often slip away to the wilderness to pray."

Was Jesus being callous? Didn't He care about these people? Don't you think they were disappointed when the Son of God took off, leaving them behind? This multitude of needy souls had come to see Jesus and not only did He not speak to them, but He didn't even offer an explanation as to why He was leaving. On the surface of things, it would appear that Jesus was being insensitive and even... selfish.

It's not that Jesus was being selfish. He was being Self-aware. He knew when it was time to retreat from the crowds in order to be still in the renewing presence of His Abba Father. Because of His practice of communion and His dependency upon God, Jesus could sense his need to hear anew from His Father in His prayer closet of the wilderness. This was Jesus' balance. He would be still in the presence of God, away from everyone. But it was precisely this stillness that empowered Him for His ministry to the multitudes.

What does the Bible say about loving others? Does it say, "Love others no matter what the cost, even if our own life goes down the tubes?" No, the Scripture says, "Love your neighbor AS YOURSELF" (Mark 12:31). Now tell me, how on earth can we effectively *love our neighbor as ourself* if we have not learned HOW to love ourself? The answer is simple - we can't. And what better way could we begin loving ourself than to commune with God in quietness, in an intimate growing relationship, so we might learn to love others with the same love He loves us with? Solitude allows our own cup to be filled in the presence of God, and in turn we can be poured out for others. This is a holy self-awareness that balances our lives between activity and solitude, benefiting us personally and allowing us to be at our full potential to benefit others.

When Jesus "slipped away" from the crowds in order to be alone in the renewing presence of God (Scripture says He "*often*" slipped away), I believe He was simply paying attention to His Own inner balance, the hub of the wheel of His life. Jesus would minister to the multitudes but, when He sensed it was time to get away, and get renewed, filled, and directed in solitude, He headed straight for the presence of God. He didn't feel the need to give explanations and apologies. He knew that without His solitude with His Father He would have nothing to give to the multitudes. By being faithful in His solitude, Jesus was being faithful to those He ministered to.

May God give us this same wisdom for our lives.

The more I look at this verse, the more I see how this was a habit of Jesus', slipping away for time to be alone. He seems to have felt comfortable with being able to distance Himself from things in order to have time in renewal with God.

Our own solitude is equally vital for our lives and walk with God, just as Jesus' was to His. When we enter God's presence, we see Him as He is, we see what He has done for us, and we praise Him. In the experience of His presence, He renews us. In stillness He reveals His nature to us and we begin to see our own new nature in Him. Out of this experience of being filled we are prepared with strength from God's presence to reach out to others in need. This is how being in touch with the "hub" of our life in God actually makes us more effective in all of the "spokes" of our life with others. God's presence provides us with a healthy balance of being in this world while living in the kingdom of God.

The Christian who has yet to find his or her prayer closet will most likely be continually at a disadvantage when it comes to giving more than pat answers to the problems of life. The person who has not yet learned the benefit of quietness may feel compelled to be in a constant state of activity, perhaps using this activity as a way of hiding from a poor self- image. But in the practice of solitude we are continually brought to the awareness of God's personal love, and this breaks the chains of suffering which a poor self-image causes. In solitude with Abba Father we are able to possess and maintain a well rounded healthy self-image.

It is, of course, a great privilege to be actively involved in the work of the great commission (Mark 16:15); going into all the

THE SOLITUDE OF JESUS

world (your immediate world) with the good news of God's love and forgiveness in Jesus Christ. To do this we must be available to those around us. We should not use solitude as an excuse to avoid contact with the world in which we live. Before we do go into all the world though, we must be convinced that in order to give to those around us, we need to be receiving from the Lord in quietness. To give out we must first take in. Our faucet may be wide open but if the water isn't flowing in then it won't be able to flow out. If our own cup is empty then we will only be able to give out emptiness.

How many in positions of ministry have "burnt-out" precisely because they didn't give heed to this most basic truth? How many Christians live the awful paradox of wanting, with all their hearts, to serve God and yet are continually feeling they are never good enough? They do more, and more, and more, and never experience the peace they are seeking. How unfortunately common it is to get caught up in the Christian rat race of working ourselves right into despair, all in the name of serving God. In this mentality, our never ending efforts can actually create a wall, blocking us from being able to relate to Jesus in solitude at all. We're too busy (like Martha) to take the time to sit at the feet of Jesus (like Mary).

In a sense, our true work is to *rest* in solitude, for out of this practice we receive the wisdom and strength needed for our work in this world. In order to serve our Savior, we must first know our Savior, or we just might wind up trying to do that which the Savior never asked us to do in the first place. To understand the mind of Christ we need to be still, meditating upon Him in His presence. As we do this His mind becomes indelibly marked upon our spirit.

We can so often be like an impatient child, trying to put his bicycle together. Instead of taking the time to thoroughly acquaint himself with the directions, because of his impatience or an assumption that he already knows what needs to be done, he dives in and becomes totally exasperated when everything he does seems to go wrong. If he would only have taken the time to calmly look at the designer's plan, he would have realized the correct steps of construction. Rather than being frustrated, he would have saved himself a lot of grief and would have experienced the fulfillment and satisfaction of a job well done.

When we remember to keep our solitude with God fresh and flowing, even if it means leaving a big crowd in order to have that quality time alone with God, we are taking the time to see our Designer's plan, so to speak. Being alone with God helps our concerns fall by the wayside. In the stillness of His presence,

His gentle blowing speaks to us and nurtures us. Instead of trying to do our work without looking at the directions, we can go forth in our work having spent blessed time in communion with our Director.

It is possible that many have tried to live the Christian life when, in fact, no one has ever shown them what the Christian life, in Jesus Christ, is. If we do not take the time to understand our Designer's plan for us it becomes so easy to fall into the trap of running full tilt in the spiritual rat race, assuming all work done for God must be good work. It's so easy to unknowingly adopt a preconceived notion about being a "good" Christian, through our obedience and works, even though the Bible emphatically states that, apart from Him (His presence), we can do nothing (John 15: 5).

In his tremendous book, "Victory In Christ," Charles Trumbull stated that the greatest heresy in the church today is "The Christian trying to live the Christian life." We would all do well to understand the meaning of this before we go running off on our own quest to become the sinlessly perfect believer. Are we supposed to "try" to be good Christians or are we supposed to "let" Christ live His life through us? Is our life dependent upon our efforts or upon His working in us?

This thought is expressed in Paul's letter

to the Philippians, where he wrote, "Work out your salvation with fear and trembling; for it is God Who is at work in you, both to will and to work for His good pleasure" (2:12-13). Most times I've heard this verse preached, it has been works-oriented ministers screaming the first half of this Scripture from the pulpit. "Work out your salvation with fear and trembling," they say. Then they present the Christian life as being totally dependent and centered upon your behavior rather than upon the Person of Jesus Christ. In this thinking, if Joe Christian obeys the laws he will be blessed but, if he steps out of line, then the merciful Jesus Who saved him just might whack him over the head into next week with His celestial baseball bat. In this type of environment the fear of God's wrath is used to manipulate obedience and "good" Christian conduct. Is this a contradictory God or what?

However, when we take the time to examine this entire verse, we see Paul was stating the exact opposite of what these preachers have concluded. According to Paul, *our* work is to let God do *His* work. "For it is God Who is at work in you, both to will and to work for His good pleasure." Who is the one willing and working for His good pleasure? Is it us or is it God? Your answer to this question determines whether your life will revolve around you or around Him. If you feel that you're the one doing all the work, in time you might become another casualty in the heap of burnt-out believers. But, if you know that He is doing the work, you will be able to rest in His goodness, living the life of joyful radiance Jesus promised to all who come to Him.

This is just one example of how blessed we become when we learn to take the time to be still and know He is God. How can we hope to know who we are in Him if we won't take the time to listen? And, do you know what? When we stop trying so hard to do God's work, we find He does a much better job of it. In solitude we are able to see what we should do and what we shouldn't do. There were times when Jesus was led to minister to people and there were times when He was led to withdraw from people. We need this wisdom that solitude provides for our own lives.

If you have the habit of assuming every need dropped into your lap is God's way of speaking to you, then in hardly no time at all you may become the type of Christian who compulsively tries to do everything and, in the process, becomes increasingly out of touch with God. The harder you work, the angrier you may actually get.

Just because an opportunity exists, it doesn't mean you must, as a "good" Christian, rise up and take advantage of that opportunity.

Just because a door opens, it doesn't mean you have to walk through it. Just because someone expresses a need, it doesn't mean you are duty bound to meet that need, regardless of what it may do to your life.

There are times when it is spiritual to get away from the crowd in order to be recharged in your own "Holy of Holies." You really are loving others when you get away and get alone with God. As you learn to practice the blessed art of bathing your spirit in the quiet awareness of His love, you will begin to evolve into the type of individual whose chief delight is to bathe God, and humanity, in the love with which He has loved you. The revelation of the Savior's heart attitude towards you, discovered in solitude, will give you the Savior's heart attitude and wisdom towards the world around you. By receiving the quiet unfolding influence of God's love, you will be enabled, in the best possible way, to "love your neighbor as yourself."

Jesus knew the difference between hearing the voice of God and hearing the voice of expectations. What this translated into, in this case from Luke, was Jesus slipping away from an awaiting crowd. Notice again the phrase "slip away." This means Jesus did not feel obligated to explain to everyone that He was tired, needed time alone, and hoped no one would be offended. He simply left them, without a good-bye and without an explanation. The Son of God knew where ministry ended and where solitude began.

May God show us this dividing line in our own lives. May He reveal to us when we need to be with the multitude and when we need to get away from the multitude.

I encourage you to make time for a "wilderness get-away" in your life. It may be a specific place where you go for solitude or it may be a time you dedicate to the Lord, even if it means locking yourself in your bedroom (your prayer closet). In time you will be able to block out the world at a moment's notice and enter the heavenlies, regardless of where you are, standing on a mountain top or sitting in a subway.

If you want your work to be truly effective, and if you want to *enjoy* what you do in God's service, then value your solitude. If Jesus needed quietness with the Father, so much that He could turn away from an expectant crowd, then how much more do we need it?

CHAPTER 4

ACTING VS. REACTING

Solitude gives us the wisdom, power and compassion to act, rather than react, to life's challenges.

"A gentle answer turns away wrath, but a harsh word stirs up anger."
Proverbs 15:1

"A soft tongue breaks the bone."
Proverbs 25:15

"He who is slow to anger is better than the mighty, and he who rules his spirit, than he who captures a city."
Proverbs 16: 32

"He who restrains his words has knowledge, and he who has a cool spirit is a man of understanding."
Proverbs 17: 27

"He who gives an answer before he hears, it is folly and shame to him."
Proverbs 18: 13

"Do not judge lest you be judged.

For in the way you judge, you will be judged; and by your standard of measure, it will be measured to you.

And why do you look at the speck that is in your brother's eye, but do not notice the log that is in your own eye?

Or how can you say to your brother, 'Let me take the speck out of your eye,' and behold, the log is in your own eye?"
Matthew 7: 1-4

"Be anxious for nothing, but in everything by prayer and supplication with thanksgiving let your requests be made known to God.

And the peace of God, which surpasses all comprehension, shall guard your hearts and your minds in Christ Jesus.

Finally, brethren, whatever is true, whatever is honorable, whatever is right, whatever is pure, whatever is lovely, whatever is of good repute, if there is anything worthy of praise, let your mind dwell on these things.

The things you have learned and received and heard and seen in me, practice these things; and the God of peace shall be with you."

Philippians 4: 6-9

ACTING VS. REACTING

"They themselves were filled with rage, and discussed together what they might do to Jesus. And it was at this time that He went off to the mountain to pray, and He spent the whole night in prayer to God."
Luke 6: 11-12

How often do we react when, in fact, we would be far better off if we acted?

Someone becomes angry with us and, instead of acting from a position of strength and understanding, we simply and naturally react to what was said by replying with our own anger. We don't really mean what we say. We might actually want to say something quite different. Nevertheless, those hot and bitter words come flowing out in a vicious torrent that surprises even us. In that moment we become a victim, not of someone else's anger, but of our own feelings and emotions. We have let ourselves be ruled by our own reaction.

If somebody casually drops a thoughtless word to us, which they promptly forget, but we have that word festering away in us for months, who has created the suffering here? Is it the person who said the word or are we the responsible party? By reacting, instead of acting, we often become our own worst enemy.

So many marriages run into trouble when the partners degenerate into a pattern of reacting off of one another. Instead of taking a word said in anger and creatively acting with it, our natural tendency seems to be to react with hurt and anger of our own. Instead of living in a trusting knowledge of each other's strengths, vulnerabilities and goodness, we mistrust and attack because of OUR own inner fears and weaknesses. "A gentle answer turns away wrath" (Proverbs 15:1). This word from Proverbs shows us how acting, rather than reacting, can dramatically change and diffuse a potentially volatile situation.

Reacting is when we take something personally and we let our response be governed by our affected emotions. Acting is not responding in kind to a thing said or done. Acting sees above and beyond the surface situation into the heart of the matter.

When we react we are considering our feelings, whereas acting is looking at other's feelings with the same compassion Christ sees us with.

Reacting is seeking to be understood while acting is wanting to understand. Acting is free

THE SOLITUDE OF JESUS

from the bondage of reaction and is able to creatively speak a word of life where we may have once instead compulsively spoken harsh and damaging words.

Acting is eating from the tree of life while reacting is eating from the tree of the knowledge of good and evil. Acting seeks the way of love whereas reacting seeks only its own justification and retribution.

Acting necessitates having a strong personal identity in Christ, which is developed in solitude. If we know who we are in the Lord then we are not likely to be shaken by someone else's opinion of us. As we live in the reality of God's love, we discover His total acceptance of us working into our innermost being, healing us of our fears and insecurities. Each day becomes an opportunity for us to see how living in the love of God affects every aspect of our lives. As we practice God's presence in solitude, a new strength and compassion is found. In the same way God has healed our inner fears, we begin to recognize this is what others need as well. In this sure knowledge of our identity as His beloved child, we are given the ability and desire to act creatively in the types of situations where we would have formerly reacted and perhaps compounded our problems.

Nobody needs to learn how to react. This

is part of the old Adamic nature each of us came into this world with. Do you remember the account in Genesis where God appeared in the garden after Adam and Eve had eaten of the forbidden tree? When God asked Adam what he had done, what was Adam's response? Did Adam act, confess his sin, and seek reconciliation with God? No, Adam reacted and said, "The woman whom THOU gavest to be with me, she gave me from the tree, and I ate" (Genesis 3:12). Adam denied his sin and in doing so blamed his actions upon his wife AND upon God. Instead of acting and restoring fellowship, Adam reacted, projected his own sin onto God and in doing so made his situation worse. The habit of reaction was born at that moment and it has been man's most natural response to life ever since.

Reacting is as easy as falling off a log whereas acting is an acquired art. Reacting is born in our weakness and fear but acting comes from the realization of our inner strength and wisdom in Christ.

In order to act we must realize there is a choice to be made. In any given situation there are emotional options open to us. We can personalize things, holding onto the hurt we feel, which is one kind of choice. Or we can choose to behold the other's hurt. We can react in our weakness or we can act in our strength.

THE SOLITUDE OF JESUS

We can be self-centered or we can be Christ-centered.

In my counseling ministry I have encountered many individuals over the years who have let their lives become completely controlled by their own destructive patterns of reaction. I have also counseled with folks who have been willing to transcend this narrow view of life. They have accepted the fact that they are responsible for their own happiness in the Lord and have entered into the healing love of Christ.

However, there are also those who steadfastly refuse to see their part in things, no matter how overwhelming the evidence of their own self-defeating behavior may be. God is ready to lovingly heal them but they are unable or unwilling to face the pain of changing their outlook on life. They are unhappy, but in their minds they have vindicated themselves and are holding the entire world responsible for their misery. Having grown used to comforting themselves through self-pity they simply do not want to see they are the ones in need of change. They constantly complain about everyone and everything. Their whole life consists of making mountains out of molehills. Ninety nine wonderful things could happen but it'll be that one sour note that will occupy their thoughts.

If only these folks could know the joys of God's presence.

ACTING VS. REACTING

In his New Testament letter, James wrote, "Let everyone be quick to hear, slow to speak and slow to anger" (1:20). In order to be able to hear it is essential that we practice the art of solitude. In solitude we can silence the many voices that shout at us everyday. In this silence we begin to truly hear with the ear of our spirit. In solitude we tune all other voices out and, instead, draw our attention inward and upward to the still small voice of God. In the quietness of God our problems recede from the shore of our consciousness and they are replaced with the knowledge of who we are in Jesus Christ. Our tendency to react is examined and our weakness exposed in the merciful light of God's healing presence. Instead of mentally crucifying the other, we realize we need to ask God to forgive US for reacting with anger, bitterness and self-pity. In our cleansing, the log is removed from our eye and we are able to correctly see whether there be any mote in another (Matthew 7: 1-5). If so, we can then pray for the wisdom and compassion of Christ to be upon that individual or situation. Solitude lets us begin acting from a position of strength. Only in solitude are we quiet enough to receive this insight from our "Wonderful Counselor" (Isaiah 9:6).

In the 6th chapter of Luke's Gospel, we are told of a time when Jesus was verbally attacked

THE SOLITUDE OF JESUS

by some Pharisees, all because He violated their understanding of the law by performing a miracle of healing on the Sabbath. Responding to Jesus' healing, Scripture says, "But they themselves were filled with rage, and discussed together what they might do to Him" (verse 11). Did the Pharisees act, or did they react? They reacted. They were actually offended by this miracle! Instead of seeing a body restored and a broken life made whole, all they were able to see was Jesus disregarding their understanding of the Sabbath. The Pharisees' reaction warped their perspective to such a degree that they actually took this miracle of healing as an insult to their faith. This example shows us how reacting can completely blind us.

What did Jesus do? Did He react to the Pharisees' rage? Did he get Himself involved in a personal argument with them? Did He become fearful of their schemes and as a result alter His ministry? Did He sink to their level and start thinking about how He could take His revenge upon them? No. This passage goes on to say, "And it was at this time that He went off to the mountain to pray, and He spent the whole night in prayer to God" (verse 12). Instead of reacting to this hostile environment, Jesus simply left it cold and went into solitude. Rather than get caught in the trap of leaving His vision manward, Jesus got alone and turned His consciousness Godward. He acted.

Jesus went to the mountain and prayed. He was quick to hear, slow to speak and slow to anger. He didn't ask God to bring down fire from heaven upon the Pharisees. He didn't use His prayer time to justify His position or to curse His adversaries. No, He communed with His Father and tapped into His mind for the situation.

The result of this night of communion on the mountain was that, "When day came, He called His disciples to Him; and chose twelve of them, whom He also named apostles" (verse 13). Rather than react to his confrontation with the Pharisees, Jesus took advantage of the situation to get alone with God and, as a result, He came up with one of the greatest creative actions of all time! Instead of being personally insulted by the Pharisees' accusations, Jesus looked heavenward and turned this occasion into one of life.

The beauty of Jesus' response was that, rather than go toe to toe with the Pharisees on this issue, as certainly the temptation must have been, He instead chose twelve men, commissioned them to go forth with His healing power and, in essence, He took His case directly to the people. The Pharisees could no longer look at Jesus as some isolated individual, healing on the Sabbath, because now it was

THE SOLITUDE OF JESUS

becoming clear that anyone who loved God could be a vessel for His healing power. It's one thing to discount one instance of healing, and write off the healer as some fringe lunatic. It's quite another thing to try to dismiss an entire movement of miracles.

When Jesus got alone He was able to see that the Sabbath was really not the issue. This was just the excuse the Pharisees used to condemn Him at that time. You don't see them applauding Jesus when He healed on the other six days of the week, do you? No, the issue here was whether or not Jesus was the Messiah. It was the nature of Jesus that was in question. Was this man of God or was he of the devil? Rather than try to prove Himself to a small group of people, who were already prejudiced against Him, Jesus went to the multitudes.

In a sense, the future of Christianity was decided that night in prayer. If Jesus hadn't let the Pharisees' disbelief and accusations be creatively used to bring Him to the solitude of the mountain that night, and if as a result He never chose the twelve, then it is certainly doubtful as to what the immediate future of His followers might have been. Without Matthew and John where would our Bible be? Without Peter and the others, who would have been there to carry on with the great commission?

Jesus acted, and let us not miss the fact that

it was in His practice of solitude that He received wisdom to make His decision. Once again, if Jesus needed solitude in order to receive the mind and the will of God for this situation, then what about us? This is another reason why stillness is so central and crucial to our lives in Christ, for not only does our spiritual life depend upon how well we practice God's presence, but in actuality all the decisions of our life are at stake.

What do you want for yourself? Do you want to be the type of person who reacts to everything immediately, and in doing so become your own worst enemy? Do you want to victimize yourself through self-pity and negativity? Or do you want to learn how to act creatively, with the mind of Christ, which solitude provides?

When we incorporate stillness into our lifestyle, we begin to discover the wisdom of God for our decisions. In quietness we are able to consciously receive what God has to give to us. In His presence we realize the great blessing of being able to act creatively in the conflicts of life instead of continuing in the destructive patterns of reaction. In our prayer closet we experience the joy and power which comes from knowing that when a choice must be made there is One to Whom we can go, unburden ourselves, and be renewed by His heavenly viewpoint.

As you dedicate yourself to practicing the art of being still, one blessing you will realize more and more is the power and compassion that comes from being strong enough to act, rather than react, in the midst of life's challenges.

CHAPTER 5

TO THINE OWN SELF BE TRUE

In solitude you discover your true self
and you are given the ability to thank God
for your individuality.

"Whatever things were gain to me, those things I have counted as loss for the sake of Christ.

More than that, I count all things to be loss in view of the surpassing value of knowing Christ Jesus my Lord, for Whom I have suffered the loss of all things, and count them but rubbish in order that I might gain Christ.

That I may know Him, and the power of His resurrection and the fellowship of His sufferings, being conformed to death;

In order that I may attain to the resurrection from the dead.

Not that I have already obtained it, or have already become perfect, but I press on in order that I may lay hold of that for which also I was laid hold of by Jesus Christ.

Brethren, I do not regard myself as having laid hold of it yet; but one thing I do: forgetting what lies behind and reaching forward to what lies ahead,

I press on toward the goal for the prize of the upward call of God in Christ Jesus."

Philippians 3: 7-8, 10-14

"'My thoughts are not your thoughts, neither are your ways my ways,' says the Lord.

'For as the heavens are higher than the earth, so are My ways higher than your ways, and My thoughts than your thoughts.'"

Isaiah 55: 8-9

"I will sing of lovingkindness and justice, to Thee, O Lord, I will sing praises.

I will give heed to the blameless way. I will walk within my house in the integrity of my heart."

Psalm 101: 1-2

TO THINE OWN SELF
BE TRUE

"Jesus therefore perceiving that they were
intending to come and take Him by force,
to make Him king, withdrew again to the mountain
by Himself alone."
John 6:15

Solitude meant more to Jesus than just a pleasant time of prayer with the Father. This wasn't something He chose to do when He had free time on his hands. We have already seen that it was in solitude that Jesus received strength and direction for His life and ministry. In quietness with His Father, Who sees in secret, Jesus connected with His path of life. Jesus could be in a crowd and say, "Who touched me?" (Mark 5:31), but in stillness He could discern who the twelve apostles were to be. There is something about practicing solitude that sharpens all of our senses, natural and spiritual.

When we get away from the roar of the multitudes, God's voice can be clearly understood.

I am convinced this is why God led John

the Baptist to proclaim his message in the wilderness. To the rational mind of that day, Jerusalem would have been the sensible spot to kick off John's campaign. Jerusalem was where it was at. Stand on any street corner and you could instantly have the ear of Jews from every part of Israel. But the wilderness - who would hear John there?

As it turned out, the wilderness was the ideal place to begin. In Jerusalem John would have been only one of many voices espousing various causes. His message may have easily been drowned out and ignored in the tumult. But in the wilderness he was all alone and nobody would misunderstand what he was saying. Sure, it took awhile for the word to get around that this strange looking character was preaching in the desert, but the waiting in quietness was well worth it, as we see when we read the Gospel accounts. Pretty soon, people were leaving the city in order to travel to the wilderness, that they may hear John's message (Matthew 3:5). In this example we see the principle that what may seem absurd to man is often exactly what God will do.

In addition to being better for the clarity of the message, perhaps this barren wilderness was also better for John, personally. This environment became an integral part of John's own identity and communion with the Lord.

THE SOLITUDE OF JESUS

Perhaps God's message was able to come through more clearly to John in the quietness of the desert. Maybe he had tried living within the congestion of the city at one time and had realized that, for him, the constant press of the crowd only hindered his ability to hear God's voice and sense His presence. Perhaps John came to the realization that he needed to escape to the quiet in order to communicate God's word to the masses.

I am convinced our own ability to receive God's personal word for our lives depends, to a great degree, upon the quality of our solitude and the type of spiritual environment we choose to live in. With so many voices crying out questions, issues and opinions at us, it is essential for our spiritual welfare that we be able to mentally break off from the noise and retreat to a place of solitude. Our practice of solitude goes hand in hand with being able to understand our identity in Christ, and remain true to it. Without the calm center of God's presence we will most likely be kept off balance in every area of our lives.

We desperately need to discern what our boundaries are. There is a time when it is good for us to be with people and there is a time when it is good for us to be alone. If we do not know when to go to the mountain and when to go to the people, we may encounter the recurring experience of being all given out with no strength left for our loved ones, for ourselves, or for God.

In the 6th chapter of John's Gospel we have another example from Jesus' life which underscores the paramount importance of solitude.

This portion of Scripture tells us about the time Jesus fed the multitudes with only a few small loaves and fishes. Now this was the type of miracle the people had been waiting for. They loved the idea that Jesus, just like the great patriarch Moses, could miraculously bring forth bread from heaven. This was the type of messiah they wanted. The multitude really didn't want to go forward with Jesus. They wanted to go back to Moses! "Evermore give us this bread," they said (verse 34). "Just keep that bread coming and we'll follow you anywhere." Jesus replied to their shallow request by saying, "You seek Me, not because you saw signs, but because you ate of the loaves and were filled" (verse 26). Jesus knew these people weren't believing in God - they were believing in bread. They didn't want to understand Jesus and His message. No, they wanted a god who would satisfy their desires and require nothing in return. Wherever Jesus went, it seems, people were always trying to make Him fit into their concept of god.

As a result of this miracle of the loaves and fishes, the people were so enthused that they wanted to take Jesus by force and crown Him king of Israel. What would have happened if Jesus had let them do this? Suppose for a moment that Jesus had accepted the crown and had been declared king by the people; then what? There would have been only one option left - war! If Jesus had gone with the expectation and pressure of the moment and accepted the crown, He would have been perceived by the Romans as yet another messianic impostor using his claims of deity in order to get an army around him. Jesus' end would have been swift, and thousands more would have died with Him. No, being made king was not a good idea, but this was the kind of here-and-now messiah the people were looking for.

So here was the dilemma. Historically speaking, this was a turning point in Jesus' ministry. On the one hand, Jesus could have given in to the demands of the multitude and gained the people's undying devotion. But in doing so He would have sacrificed His own identity, integrity and calling. On the other hand, if Jesus refused the offer of kingship, then He would risk offending the multitudes and losing their interest altogether.

What would you have done? Remember,

Jesus' ability to be the Savior of the world depended upon His sinless perfection. If He were to give in to the people here, then it would have only been a matter of time before He would have been held responsible for the murder of thousands. Roman and Israelite alike would have perished in the insurrection that would surely have been caused if Jesus had let the people crown Him king that day. His life, from the standpoint of spotless holiness, would have been rendered null and void, and we would all be hopelessly lost in our sins, apart from God.

This is, unfortunately, the type of situation so many in ministry find themselves in these days. The pressure to be all things to all people all the time and to keep everybody happy, in the final analysis, usually results in the minister losing his or her own sense of identity and value as an individual. If we succumb to the temptation to be a people pleaser then, in a very real sense, we lose our own soul.

Jesus had to make a choice. He could go with what the multitude wanted, be crowned king and, as a result, have a larger following, or He could choose to turn the people down and risk losing their affection and allegiance altogether. Recording His response, Scripture says, "Jesus therefore perceiving that they were intending to come and take Him by force, to make Him king, withdrew again to the mountain

THE SOLITUDE OF JESUS

by Himself alone" (verse 15). Once more we see Jesus acting instead of reacting. To react in this case would have been to give in to the people's wishes or reason with them or argue with them. Instead, Jesus didn't even address the issue at all. If they wanted to make Him king then that was their problem.

The way this verse from John says "withdrew AGAIN to the mountain," tells us Jesus used to do this quite a bit, doesn't it? Jesus had the blessed habit of getting away and getting quiet when the pressure was being poured on. In the solitude of the mountain, Jesus pondered the situation. He looked at the people's desire and He looked at His own priorities. On that hill, in quietness, Jesus received the wisdom He needed from His Abba Father and, as He came back down the mountain to face the crowd, He reaffirmed His own integrity to Himself and to God.

Returning from His time in solitude He confronted the multitude and in essence said, "You want bread to eat. But your minds do not yet see that I am the bread. You must be willing to eat My flesh and drink My blood or you can have nothing to do with Me" (John 6:53).

You know, Jesus could have gone soft with the crowd. He could have taken the easy way out and avoided the issue altogether. But, instead, He confronted them head on and, in very specific words, challenged them to question their own motives. His message to them was, "The party is over. It's time to choose. Do you want to follow Me? All right, but it will be on My terms and not yours." Jesus remained true to Himself. He chose, in His quietness, to let His personal integrity be more important than the size of His ministry.

Please realize that who you are is so much more important to God than what you do. Jesus said, "I will come again, and receive you to Myself; that where I am, there you may be also" (John 14:3). In other words, God cares more about your being with Him than your doing for Him. The truth of the matter is that, as we learn to "be" with Him, we are given the wisdom to know what to "do" for Him. Every time we give in to the politics and pressures of a situation, every time we compromise our integrity, we lose a little piece of our identity. Pretty soon we may have no distinct idea of who we are or what we are called to be in this world. Capitulating to the crowd and avoiding our own mountain of solitude will always keep us in a state of spiritual poverty.

This account concludes by saying, "As a result of this many of His disciples withdrew, and were not walking with Him anymore" (verse 66). On the surface it may appear as if Jesus had blown a golden opportunity but, in fact, He had

THE SOLITUDE OF JESUS

actually taken a giant step forward towards the fulfillment of God's plan for His life. "Jesus therefore said to the twelve, 'You do not want to go away also, do you?' Simon Peter answered Him, 'Lord, to whom shall we go? You have the words of eternal life. And we have believed and have come to know that You are the Holy One of God'" (verses 67-69).

Jesus may have offended and lost the support of the vast majority of His followers by being true to Himself, but to the quality people, the ones who really had hearts for God, Jesus had only grown in their estimation of Him through this confrontation. They saw the integrity and honesty of Jesus like never before. What had been a turn-off to the multitude was a shining testimony to the true disciples. Because Jesus chose to act instead of react, because He chose to affirm His identity and integrity, I believe this situation became a major turning point for the twelve. Hereafter they would be branded as the ones who chose sides with Jesus. From this time forward there could be no going back. Because He did not bow down to the expectations of others, Jesus brought life out of what seemed to be an incredibly difficult dilemma.

When peer pressure tells you to go one way, while your heart is telling you to go another, remember that remaining true to yourself will always bring out the quality people in your life. The crowds will never be satisfied. They will always want more. They will forever be convinced they know just exactly what you should do. But, as you dedicate your life to growing in God and in the knowledge of His Word, you will find that when the smoke clears there will be a small, but committed, group of true believers who will say, "We are your friends and we love you for who you are." Despite all outward circumstances, you will always be the richer as you "Walk within the integrity of your heart." (Psalm 101:2).

Before you can be true to yourself, you need to know who you are. In order to exercise integrity, you need to have a sure knowledge of your identity as a beloved child of God. I encourage you to scout out the landscape and find that mountain in the distance, that special place where you can go and commune with the Lord in quietness and confidence. As you learn to fill your heart with His renewing presence, you will become increasingly free from making choices based upon outside pressures that would wound you and have you deny who you are.

"Where I am there you may be also" (John 14: 3). This is Jesus' word to us. In stillness with Him, our senses are quieted and sharpened, allowing the clear voice of God to emerge from

THE SOLITUDE OF JESUS

the confusion that may have surrounded us. In quietness, we cease "doing" and we start "being." His thoughts become our thoughts and His ways become our ways (Isaiah 55:9). In solitude we discover our true self and we are given the ability to thank God for our individuality. Being true to ourself means knowing who we really are, a new creation, loved by God and filled with His Spirit. These are the truths that become our reality as we practice, and cherish, the surpassing value of our own communion with God.

CHAPTER 6

LISTENING FOR THE UNUSUAL

Solitude helps us understand God's word,
in the Scriptures and in our lives.

"Taking the blind man by the hand, He brought him out of the village; and after spitting on his eyes, and laying His hands upon him, He asked him, 'Do you see anything?'"

Mark 8:23

"He spat on the ground, and made clay of the spittle, and applied the clay to his eyes,

And said to him, 'Go, wash in the pool of Siloam.' And so he went away and washed, and came back seeing."

John 9: 6-7

"Do nothing from selfishness or empty conceit, but with humility of mind let each of you regard one another as more important than himself.

Have this attitude in yourselves which was also in Christ Jesus,

Who, although He existed in the form of God, did not regard equality with God a thing to be grasped,

But emptied Himself, taking the form of a bond-servant, and being made in the likeness of men.

And being found in appearance as a man, He humbled Himself by becoming obedient to the point of death, even death on a cross.

Therefore also God highly exalted Him, and bestowed upon Him that name which is above every name."

Philippians 2:3,5-9

"If then you have been raised up with Christ, keep seeking the things above, where Christ is, seated at the right hand of God.

Set your mind on the things above, not on the things that are on earth.

For you have died and your life is hidden with Christ in God.

When Christ, Who is our life, is revealed, then you also will be revealed with Him in glory."

Colossians 3: 1-4

LISTENING FOR THE UNUSUAL

"After He had sent the multitude away,
He went up to the mountain by Himself to pray;
and when it was evening, He was there alone...
And in the fourth watch of the night
He came to them, walking on the sea."
Matthew 14: 23 & 25

God can say some pretty silly sounding things. Sometimes His word may seem to be just plain ridiculous. If you didn't know better, you might even wonder if God was dealing with a full deck upstairs.

But if we do not consider, in the apparent absurdities He throws at us, what it is He is trying to communicate to us, we just may miss some of life's greatest opportunities.

Take Ezekiel for example. God told him to lay down on one side for 390 days, for a witness to Israel. Then, when he finally finished that ordeal, God told him to flip over and lay down on his other side for another 40 days (Ezekiel 4: 4-6). What if you were in the rush of traffic, trying to get to work, and God whispered that one in your ear? Would you consider, for even a second, that this was the Lord, Himself, speaking to you? Chances are you would dismiss that thought immediately.

What about the time God told Moses to stretch his staff out over the waters so they would turn to blood? How about Noah, building an ark at a time when rain was unheard of? Then there's Abraham, preparing to sacrifice his promised son on the altar at God's request. Jonah, a lone, timid man, was the one commissioned by God to preach repentance to the greatest nation on earth, the Assyrian Empire. The list goes on and on. Perhaps you're thinking, "Yes, but that was in the Old Testament."

Oh, really?

What about Joseph, hearing an angel tell him it was God Who had impregnated his betrothed, Mary? How about Peter, an expert fisherman who had come up empty after a whole night's labor, lowering his net again at Jesus' insistence? Then there's the time Peter went fishing because Jesus told him he would find his tax payment in the mouth of the first fish he'd catch.

And then there is Jesus. Time after time our Savior showed us that God's will is not always immediately understandable. Being Messiah apparently meant occasionally throwing your reputation to the wind. Listening to

THE SOLITUDE OF JESUS

the unusual seemed to be the natural way of doing things, such as, obeying God's word by: spitting in a man's face to heal him (Mark 8:23); telling waiters at a wedding to fill pots with water and that it would be turned to wine; rebuking a raging storm; raising people from the dead; walking on water; healing blind eyes with mud pies (John 9:6); and so forth.

If Jesus lived by the rational mind, He may never have performed any of these acts. He probably would have reacted to these heavenly commands like Ebenezer Scrooge from Charles Dickens classic, A Christmas Carol, when the ghost of his long deceased business partner, Jacob Marley, appeared to him. Scrooge said, "I don't believe you're real. Why, you're nothing more than a bit of undigested potato."

Let us not take Jesus' miracles for granted. Maybe we haven't considered the faith it took for Him to obey His Father in each of these things. And, therefore, maybe we haven't considered their implication for *our* lives.

What if God told you to make mud and put it in a blind man's eyes to heal him? Chances are you would reject that thought just as quick as you could. After all, there are all kinds of crazy ideas we can get. We unfortunately hear, all too often, about some group of people who are holed up in a house somewhere because they believe God told them Jesus was coming back within the week. You know, I've never been able to understand why these people always feel they have to all be in the same place. Is Jesus just coming back to their particular street address?

I remember hearing about a man once who stood in his front yard like a statue for a day because he believed God told him it would be a witness to his neighbors. I've got a feeling he might have witnessed to more pigeons than people in that one.

Then there's the trap many newborn Christians fall into of getting caught up in their zeal, but it's a zeal without wisdom. Paul wrote to the church of Rome about people who, "Have a zeal for God, but not in accordance with knowledge" (10:2). Supposing God has given them a spirit of discernment, they pass judgment on everyone who comes near them. They confuse their own mind with the mind of Christ.

This business of hearing God speak the unusual *is* full of dangers. On the one hand, we run the risk of assuming every stray thought is God talking to us. On the other hand, we run the risk of blocking out anything that sounds a little strange. How was Jesus able to tell the difference?

I think we will all agree that Jesus certainly had an advantage over us. After all, He was

THE Son of God - Deity incarnate. However, we do know that when He became flesh, He laid aside some of His power. "Although He existed in the form of God, (He) did not regard equality with God a thing to be grasped, but emptied Himself, taking the form of a bond-servant, and being made in the likeness of men" (Philippians 2: 6-7).

For instance, as we have seen, Jesus said He could do nothing independently of His Heavenly Father. In other words, He was not free to act as He wanted. He had limited knowledge and this is what made Him completely dependent upon His communion with the Father. An example of this would be the time when Jesus was asked about the date of His return. His reply was that only the Father knew (Matthew 24:36). In this way He was the same as us. Hopefully, through His example we too will learn to depend completely upon our heavenly Father, for our own knowledge is definitely limited.

On the other hand, of course, is the fact that Jesus never sinned and therefore never had a moment of broken communion with God. Jesus always desired to do God's will. He was never tripped up by His ego. So, in His thought life, He was always able to separate the wheat from the chaff, so to speak.

We are different. Our times of communion in the Spirit may certainly be outweighed by the amount of time we have lived under the influence of this world. Our minds have a whole lifetime of living outside of the presence of God. So, we are easily confused when it comes to telling the difference between God's thoughts and our thoughts.

Yes, each of us is certainly at a disadvantage if we are compared to Jesus. He almost always knew the mind of God while we seldom know it. He had a single-hearted devotion to the Father's will, while we are prone to mix in our good intentions and ideas with the will of God. Sometimes we may feel the desire to be a powerful, and perhaps famous, Christian. At other times, we may feel like we couldn't even tie our own shoes. Our thoughts are almost always throwing up a smoke screen to confuse and mislead us.

Our best safeguard in these matters is for us to know the word of God, along with the true nature and character of God. The writer of Hebrews said, "The word of God is living and active and sharper than any two-edged sword, and piercing as far as the division of soul and spirit, and able to judge the thoughts and intentions of the heart" (4:12). Knowing God's word enables us to cut away our own soulishness from His spirit. God's word, understood, enables us to separate our thoughts and intentions away from His will, leaving us with a clear focus of our Savior and our Father's direction for our lives.

If we do not know what God is like, and if we are not aware of His Personality, then I am afraid we will have a very difficult time, indeed, separating His thoughts from all the other thoughts that go coursing through our minds in any given day's time. However if we will, as Paul exhorted, "study to show ourselves approved" (2 Timothy 2:15), then we will be in the best possible place to distinguish God's voice and follow His ways.

Some Christians know little of God's true nature. Because they have not taken the time to know the Bible, in context, they are continually jumping to conclusions, saying, "God said this to me," or "God said that to me." Their religion is based more upon feelings and impressions than upon the revelation of Christ in the Scriptures. Manic-Christianity is not what God has called us to. Bug-eyed zealots who believe they have a hot-line to the Almighty have ultimately done more harm than good in this world.

The beauty of being dedicated to God in solitude is that practicing God's presence awakens our hunger to know more of Him. When we are with Him, in secret, we "Taste and see that the Lord is good" (Psalm 34:8). In my own life I've realized that being with God in solitude has encouraged me to look for Him when I read the Scriptures.

Jesus once spoke to some people about their study habits. Instead of looking for God, their studies were only making them more self-righteous and judgmental. Jesus said, "You search the Scriptures, because you think that in them you have eternal life; and it is these that bear witness of Me; and you are not willing to come to Me, that you may have life" (John 5: 39-40).

As we experience the surpassing value of living in secret with our Lord, this helps us in our study of the Scriptures. Seeing God's true nature in stillness makes us want to see God's true nature in the Bible. As we read and study we pray the Holy Spirit will quicken the word so it may "bear witness" of Christ to us. In solitude we come to Him, and Him alone, and we realize He is our life. So solitude trains us to come to Him, and Him alone, that we might have life when we study the Scriptures.

When we begin to perceive the reality of Who Jesus is, as He is revealed in the Scriptures, then we, too, are revealed. In his letter to the Colossians the apostle Paul wrote, "When Christ, Who is our life, is revealed, then you also will be revealed with Him in glory" (3:4). This verse is not speaking about the second coming of Jesus. It's talking about life here and now. As we

THE SOLITUDE OF JESUS

behold Jesus, as He becomes more and more the focus of our consciousness, then we too, as new creations, begin to be revealed. Seeing Him as He is enables us to see ourselves as we are.

As we behold our true nature in His presence old ways of thinking are replaced with a new perspective. Putting ourselves down or puffing ourselves up is replaced with the simple acknowledgment of who we are in Christ.

Going hand in hand with this new awareness is the realization that, apart from our total dependence upon Him, we could be capable of any sin or error. Walking in this humble light is the best way I know of to be able to distinguish God's voice from all others.

We can study all we want but, if we are not incorporating solitude into our own lifestyle, I'm afraid we will forever be stunted in our spiritual growth. It goes without saying that Jesus had a firm grasp of the Scriptures but let us not forget how equally important solitude was to Him. We have looked at many examples of Jesus' communion with His Father. We have seen that this is where He was able to know and be faithful to His priorities. Here is where His wisdom and direction came from. Here is where His integrity was strengthened. And, as we are about to see, here is where Jesus was able to listen for the unusual.

In Matthew's account of the miraculous

feeding of the five thousand, Scripture says, "After He sent the multitudes away, He went up to the mountain by Himself to pray; and when it was evening, He was there alone" (14:23). Once again, we see Jesus alone on the mountain, seeking God's face. He had dismissed the crowd and had sent His disciples off in a boat to the other side of The Sea Of Galilee.

What happened while Jesus spent this time in solitude on the mountain?

Going on, this passage continues, saying, "But the boat was already many stadia away from the land, battered by the waves: for the wind was contrary. And in the fourth watch of the night He came to them, walking upon the sea" (verses 24 & 25).

Jesus was alone on the mountain in prayer and it was late at night. Remember, Jesus said He could do nothing apart from His Father so, in this case, that means the Father must have said, "Go down the mountain and walk across the lake to your disciples!" I don't know about you, but I think I would have said "Are you talking to me?" I would have been able to hear God say, "It's late; why don't you get some sleep." I could go along with that. Or even, "Walk around the lake and meet your disciples when they land." That sounds reasonable. How about, "Pray that the disciples come back and pick you up?" That makes sense. But, "Walk

THE SOLITUDE OF JESUS

on the water?" I just don't think I would have immediately jumped on that one.

What I appreciate here is the fact that Jesus was in quietness when this word came. If we are in a rush and a thousand and one thoughts are racing through our minds, it's going to be next to impossible to hear the voice of God. If we are surrounded by people who are trying to enforce their own ideas upon us, as to what can or cannot be done, then it will be awfully hard to hear God say something different.

But, as you practice the art of being still, then, in that environment, you can be quiet for as long as it takes. In solitude you can hush all outside noise and give heed instead to God's voice. If you think He has spoken an unusual word to you, in solitude you can examine your own possible motives and feelings about the situation. You can be honest with yourself and with God. If you can see the redemptive value in carrying through His word, then you can more readily accept it. In quietness you are able to listen to and discern the unusual.

I am glad to see that Jesus needed quietness in order to know God's will. This encourages me because so many times I'm not sure at all about what God's will is in a particular situation. From observing the lifestyle of Jesus though, I have come to know that when wisdom is needed, that's the time to go into my prayer closet. In entering the presence of God, my emotions are examined. I quiet down and begin to see things from God's viewpoint. My own needs and desires diminish as the heart of God comes into view. His word becomes my direction, while my own misleading feelings are put in their place. The more I practice the presence of God, the more I realize just how much my entire life hinges upon my time alone with Him.

Someone once said that God cannot perform the supernatural in our lives if we only do what we ourselves are capable of doing. As long as we play it safe we may have a reasonably satisfying and effective Christianity. Yet I am convinced there comes a time in everyone's life when we are called to listen for the supernatural. God purposely utters the unusual in our ear because He knows our true potential in Him. He whispers the absurd to cause us, like Abraham, to leave our city not knowing wither we goest. It is often in this act of trusting God's wisdom over our own that we, at last, embark upon the path of resurrection life.

For sure, there will always be those who crave the supernatural in an ego-centered way. Others will wind up trying to manufacture miracles out of their own willpower and imagination. Don't let their example dissuade you from being aware of your own potential. There will be still others who will completely dismiss the supernatural as being nothing more than a mental illusion, but don't let them obscure the real thing in your life.

Listen to God. Listen long and listen in love. The more you become acquainted with your Savior and your Heavenly Father in solitude, the more clearly you will be able to hear God's voice of direction for your life. And, as you listen, you just may hear the prophetic word of Isaiah being fulfilled in you that says, "Your eyes will behold your Teacher. And your ears will hear a word behind you, 'This is the way, walk in it'" (30: 20-21).

"Jesus took with Him Peter and James and John, and brought them up to a high mountain by themselves.
And He was transfigured before them;

And His garments became radiant and exceedingly white, as no launderer on earth can whiten them.

And Elijah appeared to them along with Moses; and they were talking with Jesus.

And Peter answered and said to Jesus, 'Rabbi, it is good for us to be here; and let us make three tabernacles, one for You, and one for Moses, and one for Elijah.'

For he did not know what to answer; for they became terrified.

Then a cloud formed, overshadowing them, and a voice came out of the cloud, 'This is My Beloved Son, listen to Him!'

And all at once they looked around and saw no one with them anymore, except Jesus alone."

Mark 9: 2-8